Wednesday's Wisdom

a guide to 52 weeks of personal growth

Robin Anderson
MS Ed, CPCC
Certified Life Coach

Published by Another 8 Hours Publishing
A division of Another 8 Hours, Inc.
O'Fallon, IL 62269
http://www.Another8Hours.com

Copyright © 2018 Robin Anderson

All rights reserved.

This book may not be reproduced in whole or in part, stored in a retrieval system, or transmitted in any form or by any means — electronic, mechanical, or other — without written permission from the publisher, except by a reviewer, who may quote brief passages in a review.

Library of Congress Control Number: 2017964144
Anderson, Robin

Design and typography
by Vincent Chavez
Clean and Simple Studios
www.cleanandsimplestudios.com

First printing January, 2018
ISBN 978-0-9967202-0-5
       0-9667202-0-0

Printed in the United States of America

To Linda and Beth, who left the party too soon.

"We meet but briefly in life,
if we touch each other with stardust —
that is everything."

Unknown

Roadmap For a Wildly Fulfilling Life

1. Welcome Possibilities
2. Be Ready to Let Go
3. Give Thanks for the Unpleasantness
4. Accept Compliments Graciously
5. Do What You Can with What You've Got
6. Embrace Your Do-Over's
7. Don't Put Off Things in Your Life
8. Say Farewell to the Past
9. Create a Sanctuary
10. Do Something that Makes You Happy
11. Slow Down to Catch Up
12. Spring Clean Your Life
13. Believe You're Good Enough
14. Learn from What Annoys You
15. Check What's in Your Reflection
16. Damn "What If"
17. Put on Your Party Pants and Celebrate
18. Be Like Everyone Else, but Different
19. Be Bigger than Your To-do List
20. Kiss Envy Goodbye
21. Live Your Life Forward
22. Don't Sit on Your "But's"
23. Live with No Regrets
24. Apologize, but Not Too Much
25. Relinquish Your Whip
26. Shift Your Perspective
27. Select Passion over Purpose
28. Be Here, Now
29. Choose What Really Matters
30. Reclaim Your Power
31. Do One Thing Everyday that Scares You
32. Invite Fun, Play, and Foolishness into Your Life
33. Use Your Values as Guideposts
34. Deal with It Now or Play Whack-a-Mole with the Lesson
35. Seek Opportunities
36. Simplify Your Life
37. Establish Personal Boundaries
38. Let Go of Worry
39. Manage Your Inner Critic
40. Give Thanks, Often
41. See Every Exit as an Entry
42. Say No to Gossip
43. Intentionally Scare Yourself
44. Wake Up with a Smile on Your Face
45. Practice Civility
46. Live without Expectations or Resentment
47. Dare to be Yourself
48. Recharge Your Batteries
49. Kiss "Should" Goodbye
50. Draw a Line in the Sand
51. Awaken Your Inner Child
52. Bid Adieu to the Old Year
53. Set Intentions for the New Year

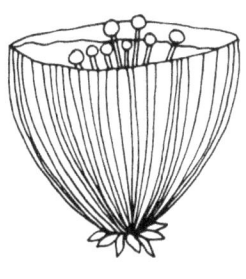

INTRODUCTION

I have always had an interest in personal development, seeking greater awareness of who I really am and what I truly want in my life. This personal quest eventually led to a career as a life coach, helping others learn these truths about themselves.

Along the way I recognized that I could reach more people—women and men—seeking such a personal exploration, so I began writing a blog on a variety of personal development topics. Over time these early writings evolved into my *Wednesday's Wisdom* blog.

My goal with this blog was not just to speak out into the ether but to offer a thought-provoking story readers could relate to, which could jolt them into a new awareness. And to ensure that the "aha" stuck with them, each entry included ways to apply and integrate the learning in their daily lives. This has become my way of offering accessible life coaching in small doses.

Overwhelmingly my readers have been grateful for the frequent nudge to take time to reflect, even in their all too busy lives. Many have shared how much the blog makes them think or offers them a different perspective on aspects of their lives. And others have thanked me for giving them the kick in the butt they desperately needed at that moment.

This book is an attempt to consolidate the best of these blogs into a format that can be used throughout a year, to be a gentle nudge to personal growth, in small doses. This book is not the usual self-help format because it does not offer advice on what you "should" do. Rather, I see it offering possibilities, consideration of new perspectives, and a place for gratitude and reflection.

If you could choose to live your most fulfilling life, would you? Of course you would. Who would turn down such an offer? Life is short. Why not create a wildly fulfilling life now?

Whatever your starting point, this book is meant to help you on your journey. I pose thought-provoking questions, offer reflective opportunities, and get you into action. Your job is to be willing to explore and to be open and receptive.

How to Use This Book
How you use this book can be tailored, depending on what you need or you want to discover. There is no requirement to read it from cover to cover, although you can do that. Here are some alternative ideas you might consider:
* Randomly open the book and see what message is waiting for you on the page you select.
* Follow the weeks, in order, recording your responses and thoughts in the book or in your journal.
* Select a particular topic that calls to you. Then see where it leads you.
* Invent your own way!

The important thing to remember is that this is *your* journey; you are in charge of the process and how you will use what you discover about yourself here. I am merely inviting you to begin your personal, self-discovery journey, notice where it leads, while enjoying the ride.

There are 52 weeks of wisdom, designed to be digested in any order that works for you. The first and last entries open and end the year so you might want to do them at the beginning and end of your exploration. Each pearl of wisdom is brief, followed by a section called, *Now It's Your Turn*, which will provide an invitation to apply the wisdom to your own life. What better way to make the wisdom stick?

The format I have chosen should invite you to participate regularly, rather than become yet one more thing to add to an already overly busy life. This is personal growth offered in bite-sized pieces! This is about allowing yourself to explore, to be curious about how things are working in your life. This is also about setting an intention to devote time to self-discovery and having the courage to incorporate what you learn.

Roadmap for a Wildly Fulfilling Life
A funny thing happened on the way to writing this book. I discovered that many of the individual blog titles fit into a framework for living an intentional, satisfying life. Hence the *Roadmap for a Wildly Fulfilling Life*. I think it is a useful, standalone guide, written as action items, that will be something to stimulate you throughout a year of personal growth.

It can also serve as a shorthand reminder of how you might want to be in the world. The *Roadmap* can help you be true to yourself, minimize your stress, experience more fun and joy, be confident with your inner compass, and improve your relationships with others. And as a roadmap, it will show you how to get from where you are now, to where you want to be.

Reflective Moments
These moments are sprinkled throughout the book to help you fully reflect on your discoveries and desires, as well as the things that don't work or you wished you had done better. Reflection will help you listen to your heart so you can better discover your true voice and your deepest desires for a fulfilling life. And the moments will

help you determine what you need to let go of or change because of who you are now.

Plan on sitting quietly for at least 10 minutes in a place where you will not be interrupted by people or technology. You want to feel comfortable so you can devote your full attention to the reflective questions. And in case you have forgotten, *it is not selfish to spend time on you*. This is about really getting acquainted with the *inner you*, the *private you*, the one you may not show to the outside world. By spending time with her, you will learn your basic truths, better know what you want in life, and find the power to allow these truths to manifest.

My hope is that by using the blog entries, and the reflection pages, you will discover a more satisfying life, let go of what you no longer need, and embrace life more fully.

Gratitude Invitations

There are also opportunities for you to pause and recognize what you are grateful for in your life. I mean, how often do we do this during our week? I invite you to think about the quote that appears on the gratitude page and decide how it applies to your life. What does it prompt you to see differently? How do you feel after completing the page? What would it be like to participate in a gratitude check-in on a regular basis?

My Wish for You

My hope is that the various pieces of this book will inspire you to think of your life in a new and different way. I am offering these suggestions, a roadmap, that will lead you to a wildly fulfilling life. These ideas are drawn from my life experiences and those of my coaching clients. So, think of this as your permission slip to begin the journey, take better care of yourself, broaden your perspective, determine what is, and is not working in your life, and then make any necessary changes.

*All growth is a leap
in the dark,
a spontaneous,
unpremeditated act
without benefit
of experience.*

Henry Miller

Week 1
Welcome Possibilities

> "To explore what it would mean to live fully,
> sensually alive and passionately on purpose,
> I have to drop my preconceived ideas of
> who I am and what I am."
>
> Dawna Markova

Can you feel it? The stillness before the whoosh. The sense of anticipation. The newness of the beginning. The bright, shiny New Year is here. And with it come resolutions and longing and hope.

Let's look forward and put your own definition of the possibilities for this uncharted New Year by asking, **What is it that will make you most fulfilled in the next 365 days?**

Fulfillment means being fully alive, a wonderful state of being because you can constantly replenish it. The true gift that keeps on giving! Fulfillment also means living a life of no regrets, where we choose **our** voice over the advice of others.

It's satisfaction and harmony in *all aspects* of our lives because we are choosing what is right *for us*. (Adios to those outside voices.) Everything in life feels properly aligned. We feel whole, honoring our values on a daily basis.

The good news (and the bad) is that it means something different to each of us. We can't clone someone else's fulfillment. There is no magic recipe and it is definitely **not** one size fits all. So, we need to define what being fully alive means *for ourselves*. But where to start?

Our sense of fulfillment is based on the choices we make, always. We can choose to move toward a deeply satisfying life or choose to veer from it. And remember: doing nothing to change what bugs us in our current situation is a choice, too.

This New Year's challenge is to choose fulfillment, to fully express who you are deep down inside, and make choices that are right for you, where you are in your life right now. Pledge to do what is necessary to be fully alive in this New Year! And unlike resolutions that disappear around mid-February, choosing to live fully happens one choice at a time, *all year long*.

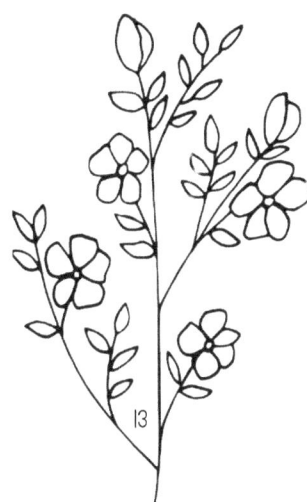

Now It's Your Turn:

How can you most honor your values in the coming year?

What first step will you take to create more harmony in your life?

What is your heart telling you that you *must* do this year?

How will you manifest the pull you are feeling in your life?

Week 2
Be Ready to Let Go

"To bear a grudge means to carry anger from the past into the present, restricting space for love, happiness, friendship and all other things that are important to us in life...and why would we ever want to do that?"

Andy Puddicombe

There's always someone who harps on and on about the harm that was done to them. They replay the hurt and the anger to anyone who will listen, go out of their way to avoid the person who "done 'em wrong", and resent anything good that happens to that person.

Stepping back and objectively looking at that person holding a grudge we see someone who views the world as a place where people are out to get them. Where they constantly have to watch their back, just in case. A tit-for-tat environment. A very angry place. With an enormous amount of time and energy focused on what happened (or they thought happened) and its effects. So much vitality wasted on looking backwards.

Reliving past events and the animosity associated with them keeps the fire stoked and the bitterness alive. It keeps us on hyper-alert for possible future harm. Our vigilance and resentment feed on one another. Round and round we go. And to what end? It's called the past because it's over and there's nothing we can do to change those events.

However our reaction *can* be changed. Our resentment is within our control. We're letting those we begrudge take up valuable space in our head! Space we could be using for so many other things, like taking time for ourselves, expanding the happiness in our lives or just being.

Are you ready to let go, even a little?

Begin by acknowledging the feelings engendered by the event that caused your grudge but don't stay stuck with those feelings . . . then recognize the benefits of letting go of them. Name the strong emotions you're feeling and notice how they're serving you. (There must be a benefit if you still feel the resentment.) Recognize the truth in the grudge as well as the lie and how fear plays a part. What's the personal cost to continue harboring these strong emotions and what would be different if you let these feelings go?

Now It's Your Turn:

Where are you holding a grudge in your life?

Notice: how does this resentment affect you (health, behavior, energy, etc.)?

Record: take out a piece of paper and write out the strong emotions associated with the grudge. Really let it rip.

Let go: find a place where you can safely burn the paper; but before you do, say the words necessary to indicate that you are moving on. You are finished with this event and all of the feelings associated with it. Then release your resentment to the Four Winds.

Week 3
Give Thanks for the Unpleasantness

"I am grateful to life for allowing me to experience exactly what my heart needs to grow and prosper and heal."

Cheryl Richardson

When was the last time you made a conscious effort to express gratitude for the not-so-pleasant things in your life?

The fabric of your life is woven together by events "good" and "bad" (your definition), by challenges and victories, by laughter and tears—a wonderful mix of ups and downs.

Each of these rhythms in your life occurs for a purpose. Often the lesson will be apparent. Sometimes the mystery of the *why* cannot be solved, at least not yet. These variations provide contrasts to deepen our experience as humans. How can you know great joy if you haven't known great sorrow? How you can learn to cherish each moment if you have never squandered your time and then felt regret?

Life would certainly become very boring if there was no variety. If everything just moved along smoothly. Although there are rare days when you probably would wish for this!

How can you take time to give thanks for the unpleasantness that has occurred in your life? Would you actively have chosen those things? Probably not. Yet, your life is richer for them. You have survived, adapted, and developed new skills as a result.

Would you really have missed all of that?

Now It's Your Turn:

Choose an unpleasantness that's happened recently. How did you deal with it—kicking and screaming or with acceptance? Why?

What did your heart need to learn from this experience?

How can you find gratitude for the lesson?

Gratitude Exercise

"Gratitude unlocks the fullness of life. It turns what we have into enough, and more. It turns denial into acceptance, chaos to order, confusion to clarity. It can turn a meal into a feast, a house into a home, a stranger into a friend."

Melody Beattie

What fullness of life can you discover as you record your gratitude?

_____
_____
_____
_____
_____
_____
_____
_____
_____
_____
_____
_____
_____
_____
_____
_____
_____

Week 4
Accept Compliments Graciously

*"We are prepared for insults,
but compliments leave us baffled."*

Mason Cooley

Why is it so hard for some of us to accept a compliment? Why do we offer an excuse to minimize what has been said about us?

Ever said anything like these in response to a compliment? "It was nothing." "Oh, I got it on sale." "I was only doing my job." "I was lucky." And on and on and on.

Why is it so hard to believe what other people are saying about us? What is going on in our heads that causes us to discount positive feedback?

Is your Inner Critic working overtime, telling you that you don't deserve what is being said? Are you thinking, "Surely that person is just being nice and they don't really mean what they say."

It's time to stop diminishing compliments and own your accomplishments! Be appreciative and gracious. Learn to savor what you're being told and accept that someone saw something worthy to praise.

Think of a compliment as a gift and act accordingly. Allow people to offer their gift and follow it with the appropriate response, "Thank you!" Nothing more. No need for clarification. Just a simple "Thanks."

Now It's Your Turn:

Practice giving compliments to others and notice their reactions. How many downplay what you have just said?

How does that make you feel?

What can you learn from their reactions?

Week 5
Do What You Can with What You've Got

"Some people just feel the rain; others just get wet."

Roger Miller

People are really good at asking themselves, "What do I want more of?" Because we're expecting something better. But what happens when you get something you're not expecting which wasn't something better?

Let's say you've had a minor fender bender, enough so that you'll need to have some body work done on your car. Do you only see the downside, spending time on the negative aspects of the situation? It's a really easy and tempting place to go, especially since we humans have a bias for seeing the dark implications. But this kind of inner talk can lead us on a downward spiral into the land of "woe is me."

What if you recognized what you've already got instead of, "How could this have happened?"

So, here's what you've got:
- no one was hurt,
- you won't be getting a ticket,
- you were only inconvenienced.

Feel the difference here?

Yes, it's annoying that it happened. Yes, it could have been worse. And yet.

By changing your perspective and being grateful for what you already have, you can change how you handle the situation, and perhaps have a gentler view of what happened.

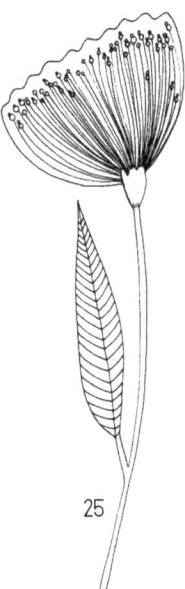

Now It's Your Turn:

Think of a recent, unexpected something that happened to you. What was your first reaction?

How did shame, blame or negative thoughts show themselves?

What different perspective might you have taken?

Week 6
Embrace Your Do-Over's

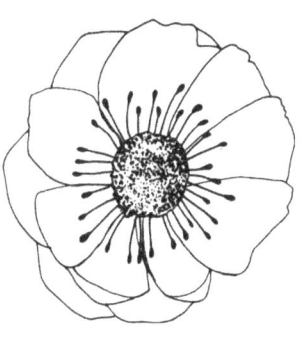

"So take a deep breath,
Pick yourself up,
Dust yourself off,
And start all over again."

Jerome Kern and Dorothy Fields

Ever beat yourself up because you slipped back into old behavior? You swore you'd never do it again . . . and yet . . . you did.

Those glorious intentions you had came from somewhere. Perhaps a deep longing for some sort of change. Or a desire to alter a habit. Or a hope that this year would be better in some way.

My guess is that your intentions got lost in the busyness of your life. And you are, after all, very human. So, put away the whip and let's refocus.

First, a reminder that an intention means you have something in mind that you are aiming for or want to effect. And intentions don't come from the realm of "should", because that's a sure sign they originated from someone else's voice rattling around in your head.

Second, make sure that your intention is truly coming from *within you.*

Third, this is your permission slip for a do-over. And do-overs don't come with guilt or self-recrimination. Yup, no whip included in this offer. A do-over just means you get to try again. No penalty box. No pointing finger. Just a simple do-over.

And I promise, you will continue to get a do-over until you finally learn what you need to learn and make the necessary change.

Now, doesn't that feel better than a guilt trip?

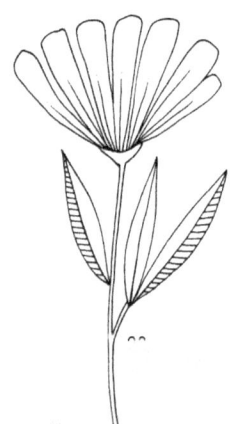

Now It's Your Turn:

How does it feel to get a do-over?

Why does this make a difference?

Reflection Moment

"Sometimes, a girl just has to dive under the duvet and regroup."

Jody Gehrman

What makes you feel as though you need to dive under the duvet? How do you know when it's safe to come out?

Week 7
Don't Put Off Things in Your Life

"Only put off until tomorrow what you are willing to die having left undone."

Pablo Picasso

The quote comes right to the point, doesn't it? Apply the quote to your life, right now. What are you putting off in your life? Maybe you're using phrases like "as soon as . . ." or "when I have more . . ."

As in, "as soon as . . . I get that new job . . . retire . . . lose 15 pounds."

Or, how about, "when I have more . . . time . . . money . . . energy."

OK, let's get real. No one knows how long they're destined to be on this earth. Your best laid plans may come to pass because you'll live long enough to see them happen.

Or not.

Are you really willing to take that chance? Do you plan to wait until you are no longer physically able to accomplish those far-off dreams? Do you want to pass from this life with regrets?

What if you planned to live every moment to the fullest? To check things off your bucket list—now. To nurture your relationships while people are still around. To seize the moment—now—because you can't see what the future holds for you.

Carpe diem!

Now It's Your Turn:

Choose one thing you're putting off because of . . . whatever. Write it here. Are you willing to die leaving that undone?

What's one thing you can do *today* to move you closer to making the thing you're putting off happen?

And when your Inner Critic pops up and tries to dissuade you, what are you going to tell it?

Week 8
Say Farewell to the Past

"I'm not the same person I was a few years ago, then why do I continue to hold onto objects that were important to me then?"

Anaïs Nin

How many things are you holding on to "just in case"? How many clothes still hang in your closet just in case you lose the weight that keeps hanging around your midsection. Or maybe you've kept those shiny stiletto heels just in case you once again go to a classy wedding? Or maybe you've hung on to those casual Friday combinations that are no longer necessary for your lifestyle?

If you're really honest with yourself, you know these likely will never happen again. And yet you cling to the possibilities.

I'll bet you're just afraid to let go of the past because these things represent parts of you, the good times, memories of who you were—back then.

Yet your past is not who you are now. True it helped you become who you are at this moment, and you need to be grateful for that. But nostalgia can weigh you down—and fill your closet. Hanging on to the past keeps you tied to what was and stifles your forward motion toward who you are becoming.

So, let go of material things from the past. Maybe even consider a farewell ceremony to mark your goodbyes. Donating these items will make you feel lighter and less encumbered, and help others who can use them.

And consciously choose to live in the now of who you are, keeping only the things that represent her.

Now It's Your Turn:

What do you hold onto that ties you to your past?

How might these things be hindering your forward progress?

Why does this make a difference?

Why is it important that old things become less and less significant as you move through your life?

Week 9
Create a Sanctuary

"I think for me home needs to be a sanctuary. I need to feel like I've escaped the day when I get home."

Belle Heathcote

Everyone needs a sanctuary, a place of refuge where we can feel at peace and recharge our batteries. We need a place where we can lose track of time and just be, without the demands and distractions of our busy lives.

A sanctuary needs to be a place that satisfies your soul, allows your eyes to feast on beauty and is comfy and cozy. A place where you can feel soothed and stress free.

Your sanctuary doesn't have to be your home. It can be anywhere that offers a private and comforting space, free of clutter and the outside mayhem. When choosing your sanctuary consider incorporating several sensory modes: sound, scent, taste, and sensual textures. And you may want to include some special treasures—but limit your choices only to items that bring you joy and brighten your mood.

The important thing is that you have a haven where you can escape to the realm of calmness, if only for a little while. Knowing that you have a readily available oasis and thinking of that space when life gets out of control, can help bring you back to feeling centered.

You deserve—and need—such a gift.

Now It's Your Turn:

What is the main characteristic you need in a sanctuary?

Why is that important to you?

If you don't already have a place of refuge, where might you create it?

If you already have one, how might you use it more often?

Almost everything will work again if you unplug it for a few minutes, including you.

Anne Lamott

Week 10
Do Something That Makes You Happy

"Always leave enough time in your life to do something that makes you happy, satisfied, even joyous."

Paul Hawken

Our lives can have so many "shoulds" and "have tos." Whether we work for someone else, for ourselves, are retired or don't work, there always seems to be something that *must* get done.

Too many of us think that we have to complete all of the "necessary" things before we can take time for ourselves. The only problem with this kind of thinking is that more and more "shoulds" and "have tos" keep appearing. And someone is often requesting our help. It seems that the faster we accomplish one thing; something rapidly takes its place.

And time for us? Never seems to happen.

But what if you took this quote to heart? What if you made sure there was *always* enough time to do something that makes you happy, satisfied, even joyous? How would your life be different?

It really doesn't require a huge amount of time or a lot of money to create some sort of enjoyment for you. That would be nice but it's certainly not necessary. I'm simply saying that you need to set aside time—surely you can spare 10 minutes—to do something that brings you joy or happiness, which sends a message to your brain that you're as important as all of the myriad things that *must* get done. It validates that you have a right to these feelings. And it creates space for your spirit to rejuvenate and breathe.

This is important.

Your contentedness, sanity, and health demand this. Because as the old commercial says, "You're worth it!"

Now It's Your Turn:

How often do you make time to experience something that makes you happy, satisfied, or even joyful?

If you feel it's not often enough, what can you do to increase the likelihood that this will happen?

What promise can you make to yourself?

Week 11
Slow Down to Catch Up

" . . . go slow to go fast . . .
that applies to everything in life . . .
If we do each thing calmly and carefully,
we will get it done quicker and with much less stress."

Viggo Mortensen

Life can feel like a treadmill on high speed; you'll never catch up. Finish one thing; three others take its place. Spinning and spinning out of control.

And so often we try to keep pace but the frustration and stress just keep mounting. We become irritable, lash out, breakdown.

Yet the way to get back on track seems an oxymoron: slow down to catch up.

We only will ever have 24 hours in a day. And speeding up to try to accomplish more will never change that fact. It will only cause us to get more wound up and frantic, spilling our stress onto others as well.

Multi-tasking is a hoax. We will never be able to adequately give our full attention to multiple things at once. So let's accept that as fact and vow to do one thing at a time.

And by slowing down, and calmly and carefully giving our attention to the one thing that needs to be done now, we can accomplish ever so much more.

Now It's Your Turn:

Where are you moving too fast?

How does that behavior affect others around you? And how do you feel about that?

What can you do to return to the person you want to be?

Week 12
Spring Clean Your Life

"Have nothing in your house that you do not know to be useful, or believe to be beautiful."

William Morris

It's a good idea to spring clean our lives, to get our internal house in order, eliminating the overload and mental and physical clutter. And once done, we can relish the uplifted spirit and permission to start again.

Look at these areas of your life to spring clean outdated beliefs and stuff that's no longer working.

1. Friends: Which friendships are stale? Or no longer provide a satisfying relationship? Who are you clinging to but have outgrown? It's time to stop dragging them around hoping things will be different. Life is too short and precious for friendships that are past their sell-by-date. Find a way to say goodbye in a way that honors both of you and what once was.

2. Money: Do money worries keep you awake at night? Do you feel stuck because of the debt that looms over you? Where have you leveraged your future to buy something you absolutely had to have? How do your spending patterns reinforce your beliefs about yourself? Seriously, do you really need every shiny, new object? Some changes to consider:

- Scale things down in your life.
- Simplify by putting less emphasis on consumption.
- Save more so you are prepared for an opportunity when it appears.
- Take pleasure in what you do own and don't compare your life to anyone else's.

3. Health: Are you happy with your physical well-being? What habits are no longer serving you? If you want to improve some aspect of your physical well-being, what is the big "Why?" What do you think you will gain by doing so? (Note that having a perfect body is not a valid answer.) Before you embark on your journey to better health, find absolute clarity on the underlying reason for doing so. You might even post it somewhere as a reminder. Find people who will support you on your journey to better health. Do this *for you*, not for the approval from others.

4. Physical Environment: What material goods no longer match the lifestyle you now have? What clothing no longer states, "This is who I am right now"? Does your home feel serene and nurturing? Time to clear out what no longer works. Clean out those closets! Keep only the things you truly love. Create a special, sacred area in your home that you can use to regroup, meditate, or just be. Then *use* this space, often.

5. Personal Growth: Time to look inward. Do you accept your complete story, the good and the not so good? Is there something about yourself that you'd rather not admit? Do you let your Inner Critic run rampant through your life? Know that you can't get rid of your Inner Critic, but you can *manage* the pesky thing. Accept that you are a good and worthy person just as you are. Embrace the "bad" bits along with the "good" ones. Your life experiences—all of them—have shaped who you are today. All of us have felt ashamed or apologized for some piece of ourselves. Now is the time to accept that you are human, one who wants to become better. (You wouldn't be reading this if it weren't true!) So, strive to love yourself, as you are. Give yourself permission to stand in the glory of who you are, and who you want to become.

6. Fun: When as the last time you had a deep belly laugh? Or deliberately chose to play? Do you often delay recreational activities until you have your work done? Maybe you feel too busy to add fun to your life? Do something enjoyable, every day. It's good for your soul and well-being. Get away from the technology in your life and find a way to allow fun back into your life. Lacking ideas? Here are some to get you started: sing (loudly) in the shower; eat your lunch outside; go for a walk and smile at everyone; take time to read the comics; put on some music and dance, dance, dance; use the swings at a playground. You get the idea.

7. Passion: Do you have something in your life that you feel passionate about? How often do you spend time on this? If you had a soapbox, what would you use it for? Do you feel your life is passing you by? Passion makes you come alive and gives your life meaning. And doing what you love gives your life purpose. Determine what special gifts you can offer to the world and then look for ways to use them. Not sure what your passion is? Recall something you did as a kid that caused you to lose track of time. Find a way to integrate that activity or feeling into your life.

Now It's Your Turn:

Pick one of the spring cleaning areas above, then schedule some time to ponder the truth of it in your life. What changes can you make in that area?

How willing are you to do so?

What is one thing you can do this week to clean out the debris there?

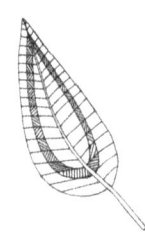

Reflection Moment

"Do not hide your light for fear of what others may think of you.
Let it shine and be a reflection of what is possible."

Kristi Bowman

How will you let your light shine? When you do, what becomes possible?

_____
_____
_____
_____
_____
_____
_____
_____
_____
_____
_____
_____
_____
_____
_____
_____
_____

Week 13
Believe You're Good Enough

*"Our deepest fear is
not that we are inadequate.
Our deepest fear is that we are powerful beyond measure."*

Marianne Williamson

We are so hard on ourselves. We compare our insides with someone else's outsides. And more often than not, we find ourselves lacking. We may head down the would-a, could-a, should-a tracks, chugging on that downward spiral. Our insecurities loom large. And it never feels very good.

So why do we go there?

Because we think we need to be like others. That we need to be the best at everything we do. We believe "they" never have self-doubt. So we compare and contrast, and find ourselves lacking.

Unfortunately our culture frowns on showing our vulnerabilities. So most people won't honestly share their fears, failures or shaky self-confidence. We wear masks, giving the impression that we're stronger than we are, or more capable, or more . . . anything.

It's important to recognize that we all want to be seen, heard and feel as if we belong. And that being the best at everything is unreasonable! So what to do?

Give up striving for perfection. Remember: for every would-a, could-a, should-a, you've got a long list of things you've done right. Congratulate yourself on being "good enough" and often, *more than good enough*, in those situations.

Now It's Your Turn:

What are your 10 best decisions?

How did you feel during those times?

What will help you remember that you **were** enough then?

Week 14
Learn from What Annoys You

"What fault of mine most nearly resembles
the one I am about to criticize?"

Marcus Aurelius

Ever been in a situation where someone is pushing your buttons? Something grates within you? What is it that creates such a powerful reaction in you?

What if what you are seeing in them—the label—really belongs to you? What if the negative attributes you so readily see in others are hidden parts of yourself, parts you refuse to acknowledge openly?

The truth is we all have a shadow self, that part of us that we believe is somehow not acceptable to others or to ourselves. So we stuff these thoughts deep down inside, and use our energy to keep them out of our sight.

Unfortunately, these characteristics refuse to stay tamped down. What you try to ignore in yourself, you readily see in others. After all, your radar is keenly set to "see" these characteristics. And, it's so much easier to project these attributes onto others than to own them within yourself.

You can run but you can't hide. These unwanted characteristics are not going away. They are part of you. So, are you forever stuck here?

Anything that is hidden away, consciously or not, has power over us. By ignoring those parts of ourselves that we find unacceptable, we are refusing to recognize all aspects that make us who we are.

Embrace yourself, the good and not so good, recognize you are a work in progress, and change the things you can.

Now It's Your Turn:

The next time someone pushes your buttons, stop and label the characteristic that is getting you riled up. What exactly is causing your discomfort?

What is the truth in how this characteristic shows up in you?

How can you accept this part of yourself?

Week 15
Check What's in Your Reflection

"Everything that happens to you is a
reflection of what you believe about yourself.
We cannot outperform our level of self-esteem.
We cannot draw to ourselves more than we think we are worth."

Iyanla Vanzant

Think back over the past week and select several things that happened to you. First notice: were there more "good" or "bad" memories? That alone should be an indication of how you view your world.

Did you first remember the things that were less than what you had desired, made you mad, caused you upset, or were painful? Or, did you recall joyful, fulfilling, fun or successful actions?

Our perspective has a major impact on how we view life and the things that happen. We can choose to view the world in a positive light—or not. And this correlates to how we perceive our own self-worth.

When you approach a situation, do you think, "I'll be OK no matter what happens." Or does this describe you: "Hope for the best but expect the worst." Do you label things that happen to you as problems or opportunities?

The way we look at life is an immediate reflection of how we view our place in the world, our power, and our self-esteem.

If we respect ourselves, possess self-confidence and trust in our ability to land on our feet no matter what, we become resilient to the events in our lives. Things no longer happen "to" us. We lose the victim mentality because we are strong and self-assured, and because *we consciously choose our reactions*.

Opportunities appear, and "problems" become challenges to learn from and overcome.

With self-respect you know what you will and will not accept in your life. You are certain that you can determine your path in life, ignoring the voices of the naysayers. You strongly believe in your own power, which gives you tenacity and courage. From this viewpoint, anything is possible!

Now It's Your Turn:

Notice your self-talk for the next week. Where do you put yourself down? Compare yourself to others? Deny your true abilities? Dilute compliments?

In each of these cases, reframe your self-talk and state your truth. Rewrite each personal put down, using this format: "No, that's not true, I really can . . ." and state the positive. What do you notice?

How can you act like you believe these statements?

After receiving a compliment say to yourself, "Yes, I really am . . ." (and fill in the same words from the compliment). Notice how changing your self-talk affects you.

*If your compassion
does not include yourself,
it is incomplete.*

Jack Kornfield

Week 16
Damn "What If"

"It ain't no use putting up
your umbrella till it rains!"

Alice Caldwell Rice

How much time do you spend in the land of "What if"? You may think this is a necessary way to be prepared for anything that might arise. So that you're not caught unawares, blindsided, or hurt.

But you know, this is just another way of saying that you worry.

How many hours have you spent planning for what may never happen, for "just in case" the sky should fall. Maybe you are waiting for the other shoe to drop.

Do you spend considerable time planning and plotting and trying to see from all possible angles? On the off chance that something that you haven't thought of just *might* occur. Do you believe that feeling prepared gives you a sense of control.

Time for a reality check. How much control do you *actually* have of the future?

Are you squandering huge heaps of energy in anticipation of something that may never happen? Are you willing to sacrifice *today's happiness* fretting over what might never occur?

What if you packed your day with truly L-I-V-I-N-G and being in the moment, dealing with whatever, *as it happens*, and not before?

What would change if you believed that you will have plenty of time and energy to deal with any problems—*if* they occur.

Now It's Your Turn:

What's your current biggest worry?

Stand on your bathroom scale and envision holding your worry in your arms. How much additional weight are you carrying? Maybe it spills over, or keeps changing shape. How does it feel in your arms?

How does this weight affect your posture?

Now imagine that you're holding your worry in your arms, hour upon hour, for one full day. What one word describes how you feel after the 24 hours?

What do you want to say to yourself?

Week 17
Put on Your Party Pants and Celebrate

"I celebrate myself, and sing myself."

Walt Whitman

It's so easy to check things off your to-do list. OK, done. Next item. Check. Done. Round and round you go.

But how often do you take the time to *intentionally* recognize what you have accomplished? This goes way beyond just making a check next to the items on your list.

So many people neglect the important step of celebrating. We just move on, looking ahead to the next thing to do. And yet we're missing the juicy part. Where we get to recognize what we have accomplished.

Often we get to the end of our day and think, "Where did the time go? I didn't get anything (or not much) done." But the truth of the matter is that we *did accomplish tasks*. While we may not have done what we wished we could have, or completed the big-ticket items, we still made progress.

Some days that's about all we can say. Our days get interrupted, our plans unravel, we get sick. Yet over the long run, we *do* make a difference. We finish the major project. We get better at something. We complete our goals.

But what we too often miss, the next important step, is to stop and then celebrate. We need to take the time to recognize where we were and where we are now—a vital step that shouldn't be glossed over.

And there are so many delicious ways to celebrate! Buying something special; taking yourself out to dinner; some time spent doing nothing; a long, hot bath. You get the idea. These suggestions are just to prime your creativity.

And while you are engaging in your celebratory activity, toast yourself intentionally, so you know just how proud you are of you. Prost!

Now It's Your Turn:

When was the last time you celebrated yourself?

List 3 big things you have accomplished. What are you especially proud of doing?

Now list 3 more mundane accomplishments. Why are you proud of these?

How can you celebrate one thing from each list?

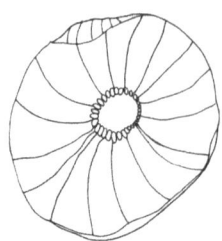

Week 18
Be like Everyone Else, but Different

"Comparison is all about conformity and competition . . .
this crushing paradox of 'fit in and stand out!'
It's not cultivate self-acceptance, belonging and authenticity;
it's be just like everyone else, but better . . ."

Brené Brown

How many times have you been caught in this web? How often have you thought, "If only I could look like, act like, have what she has, I would be happy." And in your efforts to catch up or fit in, you strive harder, often pushing way beyond your limits financially, emotionally or physically.

And what exactly do you gain by trying to be more like "them"? Maybe a sense of belonging. A feeling of acceptance and validation. Or perhaps the relief that someone else is making up the rules.

But what does this cost you? How much of your own style gets lost in the crowd? Does fitting in truly bring you happiness?

And what does the competition and comparison create in you? Probably a sense of inadequacy, of not being enough, as you are. Does that feeling really make you fulfilled?

Of course not!

In case you forgot: here's your reminder that you are unique, which already makes you special. You have special gifts and talents and experiences and perspectives. All of which allow you to make your own special contribution to the world. There is, and always will be, only one of you.

And that can be hard to remember when you get caught up in your busyness. Or when you let yourself get all tangled up, allowing self-doubt to creep in, and then once again find yourself competing with others, with you on the "losing" side.

The curious thing is that "losing" comes from within you. And its meaning always seems to change.

Do you see the absurdity here? We do this to ourselves. It's time to put an end to this self-defeating cycle. So, be like everyone else, but also be your own, different, unique self. Never lose her.

Now It's Your Turn:

List 20 ways you are unique in the world.

What are some benefits of being unique?

When do you hide your uniqueness? Why?

A New Perspective on Gratitude

Be thankful that you don't already have everything you desire,
If you did, what would there be to look forward to?

Be thankful when you don't know something
For it gives you the opportunity to learn.

Be thankful for the difficult times.
During those times you grow.

Be thankful for your limitations
Because they give you opportunities for improvement.

Be thankful for each new challenge
Because it will build your strength and character.

Be thankful for your mistakes
They will teach you valuable lessons.

Be thankful when you're tired and weary
Because it means you've made a difference.

It is easy to be thankful for the good things.
A life of rich fulfillment comes to those who are
Also thankful for the setbacks.

Gratitude can turn a negative into a positive.
Find a way to be thankful for your troubles
And they can become your blessings.

~ Author Unknown

Week 19
Be Bigger than Your To-Do List

"One day you will wake up and there won't be any more time to do the things you've always wanted to do. Do them now!"

Paulo Coelho

How often do you put off having fun or doing that thing you want do do? "Just let me finish one more thing" . . . "It's a weekday, fun happens on the weekends" . . . "As soon as . . . then I can . . ."

Most of us are guilty of this, big time. How often we get sucked into the vortex of "I have sooo much to do." And we create self-imposed pressure by never saying "NO" and just merrily expanding our to-do lists.

We create our own insanity and overwhelm. And it usually leads to a predictable crash and burn, affecting those most important in our lives and others around us. Cue the anger, frustration, tears, doom and gloom music.

How much of this distress is self-created angst, magnified by our sheer will to suck it up and get on with it? And how many of us ignore the possibility of asking for help?

Well, here's the truth: you're not getting any younger. What about all of those things you plan to get to "someday"? When is it truly going to be the "right time"? When you're physically incapable of doing the things you long to do?

This is about doing what you need to **and** doing what you want to—having a balance and stepping into the fullness of your life.

Now It's Your Turn:

What is something that you really want to experience in your life?

What is one step that you can take to bring it closer to reality?

What will help you stay in motion, enabling the experience to happen sooner, rather than later?

Week 20
Kiss Envy Goodbye

"When I realize that God makes his gifts fit each person,
there's no way I can covet what you got because it just wouldn't fit me."

William P. Smith

Ever battle the green-eyed monster? The one who preys on your insecurity, and gleefully swooshes in when you're feeling the least bit shaky about where you're heading.

This sneaky <expletive deleted> monster usually pops up whenever you're in the midst of others who seem to have it all. It nips at your ankles like a young, untrained puppy, peeing on your feet when you try to ignore it. Compare and contrast becomes your modus operandi as you concentrate on what they have.

We have such a knack for making ourselves feel inadequate. Or trying to live someone else's life.

So how do you get out of this rut?

Know your intention. Know why you're making a specific choice. Is it because it satisfies your needs or because you "have to"? Get really clear on your intention.

Know your goals. What do you want to get as a result of a specific choice? Focus on what you want, not on what they have.

Know your reality. What gifts and talents do you have, that makes you unique? The world is waiting for these talents, delivered with your own special style.

Using these 3 introspective factors will help you stay grounded in your intention, and clarify what you want, all the while appreciating your own capabilities, leaving you no desire to focus on anyone else.

Now It's Your Turn:

What causes your green-eyed monster to appear?

What can you say to this monster so it loses its power over you?

What special talents or gifts do you possess?

Week 21
Live Your Life Forward

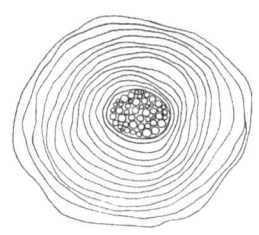

*"When a thing is done, it's done. Don't look back.
Look forward to your next objective."*

George C. Marshall

Consider your rearview mirror v. your windshield—the perfect metaphor for living your life forward.

Ever notice that while you're driving you only take an occasional glance behind while you spend most of your time looking forward through the much larger windshield? This way you can scan the horizon, watch for what is coming your way, and prepare yourself to handle whatever arises.

What would happen if you spent most of your time looking backwards, through the small, rearview mirror? You would be caught up in what has gone before, what you've moved beyond, all the while sacrificing steering where you are going.

This sounds obvious if you're driving. But isn't this often what we do with our lives?

How many times have we our spent time reviewing, reliving and trying to recreate or alter the past. All the while we are missing what is right in front of our noses. And our steering forward is hampered because our attention is focused behind us.

So it comes down to a choice: we can keep our eyes forward, directing our life as best we can, remaining open to possibilities, or we can stay focused on what was, which sends us rapidly into the land of would-a, could-a, should-a.

Now It's Your Turn:

What do you hold onto that ties you to the past?

How does fear play into this?

How would your life be different if you kept your eyes on the road, looking forward?

Reflection Moment

"Women need real moments of solitude and self-reflection to balance out how much of ourselves we give away."

Barbara De Angelis

How does reflection help balance out your life?

_____
_____
_____
_____
_____
_____
_____
_____
_____
_____
_____
_____
_____
_____
_____
_____
_____
_____

Week 22
Don't Sit on Your "But's"

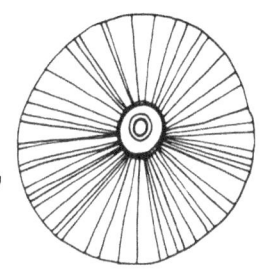

"The moment one definitely commits oneself,
then Providence moves too.
All sorts of things occur to help one
that never would have otherwise occurred."

Johann Wolfgang von Goethe

Many people say they would love to try something new . . . **but**. So often there's that awful, disconcerting . . . **but** . . .

" . . . Where would I find the money, or the time, or the energy? they say. **But** . . . I'd have to wait until this or that would happen."

And, of course, the perfect retort is: **but** . . . how long are you going wait?

What if you believed that the Universe truly is on your side, just waiting for you to take the first step? All you'd have to do is begin. And then you can take small steps or a giant leap—whatever would feel comfortable.

What if the Universe was just waiting for a nod from you?

You wouldn't have to have all the details worked out. You might not even have a clear vision of what exactly you are wanting. You could move with what you know . . . now.

The important thing is you would be moving forward, not sitting on your **but's!**

Now It's Your Turn:

Where in your life is **but** getting in the way?

What's holding you back?

If you were to take the teensiest little step forward, what would you do? What would it actually take do that itsy, bitsy step?

Week 23
Live with No Regrets

*"Regret is an appalling waste of energy,
you can't build on it—it's only good for wallowing in."*

Katherine Mansfield

Would-a, could-a, and should-a, how often have you used these words? It may have happened so many times that you no longer notice when they've been said (or thought). All 3 of them reek of "if only . . . ".

Yes, this is one way to look back on your choices, actions or thoughts. Yet, none of them can be changed. They are the past—done—a part of you, like it or not!

Regrets also can apply to choices you didn't make and now wish you had. This line of thinking may send you off with "If only I had [fill in the blank], my life would be so much [fill in the blank]."

Both situations have some things in common: they are backward looking, wishful thinking, with a dash of desire to rewrite history—yours. Interestingly, they also include a longing to have done things differently.

How about reframing those choices and actions that you took, replacing would-a, could-a, should-a with "Next time I'll..."? This creates a new perspective, causes you to build upon what you have learned, and put into practice the lessons.

And then you have to let go of the past. Done. You've learned. Now, get on with your life.

There are so many people ready and willing to beat you up in life, why should you also be one of them?

As for regret for things you never did . . . what's holding you back now? Do your desires and wants come with an expiration date? If so, who imposed it? And, more importantly whose life is it, anyway?

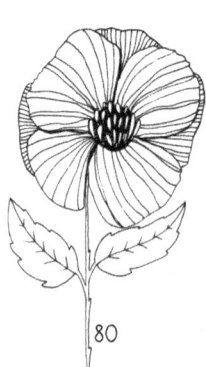

Now It's Your Turn:

What are 5 actions you can take to move you closer to a life of no regrets?

What hidden desires are rumbling around inside of you?

What would your life be like if you gave them their voice?

Week 24
Apologize, but Not Too Much

"I don't ever apologize for who I am because then I let someone else decide who I am."

Kyan Douglas

I'm sorry. Oops, sorry. I'm sooooo sorry.

Sometimes we use these phrases to avoid conflict and offset potential anger: "I'm sorry to bother you but . . ." We think this helps keep the peace and ensures that people will continue to like us. Actually, it creates an imbalance in our relationships because we are putting ourselves in a submissive position.

Or maybe we're so eager to foster cooperation and community that we apologize just so we can move on. What we're really saying is that our honesty takes a back seat to getting along.

The common denominator here is that we're giving away our power, freely and willingly. When we apologize inappropriately the implicit message is that there's something wrong with us and that we don't know what we need. We somehow don't measure up. When we do this often enough it becomes our truth.

So what's the remedy?

We need to say what we mean, without apology. Instead of "I'm sorry, I didn't hear you", try, "Would you repeat that, please?" Feel the difference?

Sure, we need to apologize but only when it is necessary. Like when we hurt or disappoint someone. And we need to stop using "sorry" as conversational filler or when we have no control over what happened.

There are great gifts waiting when we stop over-apologizing: improved self-respect and self-awareness, and more honest relationships with others.

Now It's Your Turn:

Pay attention to how often you apologize then stop and reflect on why you've said, "I'm sorry" or any of its variations.

Was the "I'm sorry" necessary or was it habit? What was your intention?

How could you have rephrased the apology so that it became a statement of what you needed?

Gratitude Exercise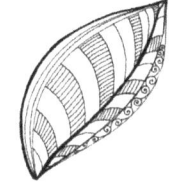

"When we focus on our gratitude,
the tide of disappointment goes out
and the tide of love rushes in."

Kristin Armstrong

What disappointment can you let go of as you focus on what you do have in your life? How can you be grateful for that disappointment?

Week 23
Relinquish Your Whip

*"Often, we are harder on ourselves than others are.
If we cannot forgive ourselves, how can we forgive other people?
(We can) learn to accept ourselves for who we are,
knowing that we can always gently work on making improvements."*

Patrick Wanis

We've all done things that we wish we hadn't. And most often they were done unintentionally. Yet we keep reliving the incident, hoping for a different outcome. And just to add salt to our wound, we begin beating on ourselves for our actions. We think, "Just one more whack with the whip and that should take care of it."

Welcome to being human!

We all make mistakes; that's the downside of being human. However, we can control our reaction to making these errors of judgment.

We can own the mistake. And we can recognize that there is nothing in our power that can change the past. It just is. So this leaves us with a choice: we can wallow and continue with the personal whipping, bleeding our regret-filled selves on those around us.

Or, we can focus on the new day, on the here and now. Because if we continue to replay that dumb thing we did, we're really not fully present in our lives. And we will miss what is happening in this moment. And the next one, and the following one.

So say goodbye to your mistake. Forgive yourself for being human. Pick through the debris for the lessons. And gratefully greet the next moment.

Now It's Your Turn:

What mistake have you been carrying around for too long?

Why does it bother you so much?

What lessons can you find in this incident and your reaction to it?

What would be a positive result of forgiving yourself for this mistake?

Week 26
Shift Your Perspective

"If you don't like something, change it;
if you can't change it, change the way you think about it."

Mary Engelbreit

Sometimes it feels as if life just wants to cause us irritation. We get stuck in unending traffic, the phone won't stop ringing, or the weather makes us late for appointments.

But what if we implemented the above quote? What if we *reframed how we view what happens to us?* There are so many things we cannot change, and yet we rail against them as if that will make a difference.

How do you react when the overnight storm means you'll have to find a different way to work? Or the skies have just decided to open up with a tremendously heavy downpour and you're wearing brand new, expensive shoes? Or your child comes home sick, meaning someone will have to stay home and play nurse. Or . . . or . . . or . . .

In all of these situations, you have a choice: take it personally, fume, and become more and more stressed, or step back and determine if there is something you actually can change about the situation. Is there anything? If the answer is, "No", then your only viable choice is to alter your perspective of what's going on.

Changing your viewpoint will shift your relation to the situation, and you'll lessen the need to feel the impulse to fight against it.

And you'll regain your serenity.

Possibilities:
* You've been given time, alone, to think because you're stalled in traffic.
* You have an excuse to go barefoot in the rain, which you loved as a child.
* You get a respite from the frantic pace in your office because you're staying home to care for your sick child.
* You have a chance to actually pay attention to your surroundings when you take that alternate route to work.

See the difference that a change in perspective makes? *We get to choose how we see the world.* We can view life as hard, everything goes wrong, woe is me . . . or we can consciously choose to find the humor, the entertainment, or an alternative way at looking at a situation.

Wanna join me in wearing a different pair of glasses?

Now It's Your Turn:

Recall a recent incident when you got all bent out of shape. How could you reframe that event?

Where was the humor, the entertainment (for you or others)? How can you laugh at yourself?

How has this changed your perspective about that incident?

Week 27
Select Passion Over Purpose

"Passion is a feeling that tells you: this is the right thing to do.
Nothing can stand in my way.
This feeling is so good that it cannot be ignored."

Wayne Dyer

There's a misconception about the need for a life purpose: it's supposed to be the golden path to feeling fulfilled *throughout your life*. Life purpose means there's only one path and your job is to find it.

The only problem is that we have many selves that make up who we are. So if we limit ourselves to just one purpose—one passion—for our *entire* life, we will miss out on so many other fulfilling ventures.

How many different roles have you had in your life? Parent? Employee? Adventurer? Writer? Artist? Gardener? Each of these passions has matched a certain period of your life. And each has fulfilled who you were *at that time*. More than likely you put your heart and soul into each passion and felt great fulfillment. And yet you probably sensed when it was time to move onto something new.

As Wayne Dyer says, passion shows up with an air of certainty about it, regardless of our Inner Critic or the voices of others. You may not know that something is going to turn into a passion—unless you try it.

Give yourself permission to follow your new bliss. Until it no longer is a passion. Who knows? Maybe this will last the rest of your lifetime. Maybe not.

Either way, let passion rule your life and revel in a feeling so good it cannot be ignored.

Now It's Your Turn:

What are you passionate about right now?

How does this give you a sense of fulfillment?

Don't have a passion? What do you really care about? Could this become a passion?

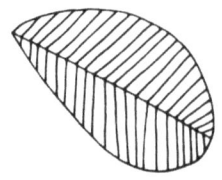

Reflection Moment

"Anybody looking for a quiet life
has picked the wrong century to be born in."

Whitaker Chambers

Why is this true and how can you counteract the fact?
_____
_____
_____
_____
_____
_____
_____
_____
_____
_____
_____
_____
_____
_____
_____
_____
_____
_____
_____
_____

Week 28
Be Here, Now

*"The world is full of magic things,
patiently waiting for our senses to grow sharper."*

W. B. Yeats

Has this ever happened to you? You're driving home, spending the time reviewing what you did/didn't accomplish on your to-do list. Add in a radio tuned to the cacophony of today's news, with your mind churning anywhere but in the moment.

Did you notice the stunning sunset? Or the light playing through the clouds? Or the sun's receding rays creating brilliant shades of yellows, then reds and oranges?

Now imagine that you had slowed down because the scene took your breath away — this was a phenomenal sunset. And you noticed that your breathing was more even, the concerns of the day, the "shoulds" were magically melting away. You recognized that you felt more centered and grateful that Nature had given you the opportunity to put things in perspective, allowing you to consciously choose to savor the moment.

As you neared your home, your only thoughts were a litany of glorious adjectives for the beauty you had just witnessed. Your worries and stresses from the day were no longer foremost on your mind. You had been in the moment, loving every second of it. What if this truly had been your reality?

Or, what if you had quickly glanced at the sunset and then gone back to your rumination, fretting that your day hadn't gone as you had wanted, and you were swirling in the past?

You *do* have a choice.

What if you really had decided to be here, now? If you had given yourself permission *to enjoy as well as to do*, to allow enough space in your life to breathe in the beauty that is ever present?

What would have been different as you walked through your front door?

Now It's Your Turn:

What would change for you if you gave yourself permission to stop and savor the moment?

Here are suggested practices for you, to help you to be in the moment. Set your alarm to sound at a random, unexpected time. When the alarm goes off, spend the next 3–5 minutes with one of these ways of being, or even better, make up one of your own!
* Listen to the sounds around you
* Breathe deeply for 10 rounds of slow breath with your eyes closed
* Leisurely register the colors and textures of your surroundings
* Concentrate solely on the beating of your heart
* Notice the various patterns of light and shadows around you

How does this exercise change you?

Week 29
Choose What Really Matters

"The whole problem with people is . . .
that they know what matters,
but they don't choose it."

Sue Monk Kidd

Do you know what *really* matters in your life? Sounds like a simple question, yet many people struggle with the answer. Or more often, don't want to think about how their actions are providing the answer.

Your words say that family and friends are the most important things to you, yet your choices tell a different story. You may spend more time on your career and outside interests than you do with those near and dear to you. You may become distracted by things because you get caught up in the drama and busyness whirling around you.

And, in the end, *this will cost you*. Relationships will wither from neglect. Friends will fade away. And then what? What will you be left with as you approach the end of your life?

If you're caught in this spiral, here's your wake-up call!

And to put it in even greater perspective, think about this: when you're on your deathbed, how much value will you put on your career, the acclaim you garnered, the successes you had? Wouldn't you rather be surrounded by family and friends, and by the people who mattered the most in your life?

So, now you have a choice. What's it going to be?

Now It's Your Turn:

Make a list of those who really matter to you in your life.

Imagine that they each have given you a grade on how important you make them feel. What would be your grades?

Are you satisfied with the result? If not, what are you going to do about it?

Week 30
Reclaim Your Power

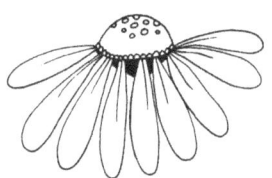

"Your time is limited; so don't waste it living someone else's life."

Steve Jobs

What do these things all have in common? Lack of self-confidence, allowing others to make all of the decisions, "going along to get along," getting caught up in other people's drama, not standing up for personal beliefs, discounting personal skills and abilities, being the "nice girl," or being fearful of appearing "selfish."

All of these situations are a direct result of giving away your personal power. Bottom line? This means *letting others determine what you think, feel, and believe, and how you behave.*

We allow these behaviors to crowd out and overwhelm our sense of self, our authenticity, and our true inner voice. In essence, we are choosing to let others run our life!

Most often, we let our sense of self-worth be defined by someone other than ourselves. The mass media influences how we feel about our weight, the wrinkles we have, or the strands of grey hair that begin to appear. We're too short, too tall, too fat, too thin, too busy, not busy enough, too selfish, and on, and on, and on. We take care of everyone at the cost of taking care of ourselves.

All of these are choices that we make. These are habits and behaviors that have become ingrained in our very being. And all of these choices come with a hefty personal price.

But here's the thing about choice: there are always options leading to action. Quite literally, to choose means to select after consideration. You can choose to believe something, or not. If something is no longer serving you—if you want back your power—you can choose to reclaim it!

Now It's Your Turn:

Where do you give away your power, to whom and under what circumstances?

What benefits—and there **are** benefits—are you getting by handing over your power to someone else?

Weigh the consequences of giving away your power against your desire for change. What do you notice?

Gratitude Exercise

"Give yourself a gift of five minutes of contemplation
in awe of everything you see around you.
Go outside and turn your attention to the many miracles around you.
This five-minute-a-day regimen of appreciation
and gratitude will help you to focus your life in awe."

Wayne Dyer

What miracles do you see around you? How can you create a five-minute-a-day gratitude regimen?

Week 31
Do One Thing Every Day That Scares You

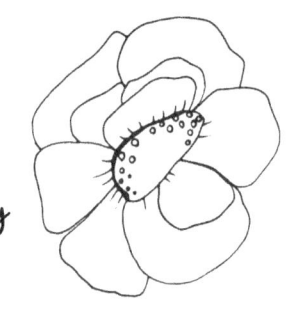

"Do one thing every day that scares you."

Eleanor Roosevelt

Courage. According to my dictionary, it's the "ability to conquer fear or despair." I believe it's about believing in oneself and leaping into the unknown, without a manual or guarantees. It's about being proactive rather than reactive.

Courage is the antidote to fear. It's like a muscle: the more you use it, the more easily it comes to you. And you can build it one small, tiny, step at a time.

No child jumps on a bicycle for the first time and rides off happily into the sunset. There are cuts, bruises, and scrapes along the way—not failure, but part of the lesson of learning to overcome the fear. The child's yearning to ride that bike diminishes any fear they may have of trying.

Where did our childhood courage go?

You remember, someone would yell, "Come on, let's do it!" and you would be off on some adventure, consequences be damned, "consequences" not being a frequent visitor in your vocabulary, much to the chagrin of your parents.

How can you recapture that independent spirit, that fearlessness? Your long-lost courage?

As Eleanor Roosevelt implies, *you need to practice*. One day at a time. Every day. And the more you practice, the less scary the unknown will appear. Small courageous acts will turn into larger ones. Your confidence will grow, shriveling self-doubt. Your "what-ifs" will become, "Oh, yeahs!"

How can you stop avoiding experiences outside your comfort zone? You can actively engage with your world, instead of letting things "happen" to you. Surround yourself with people who have faith in you and truly believe what they see there. Ensure that you give yourself credit when you take each small step. You can turn fear into a challenge and just do it.

Now It's Your Turn:

Who are 5 people who believe in you, no matter what?

How can they help you to be more courageous?

When you feel fear sneaking up on you, what can you tell yourself to feel a bit more courageous?

Week 32
Invite Fun, Play, and Foolishness Into Your Life

"Mix a little foolishness with your prudence; it's good to be silly at the right moment."

Horace

Kids love April Fool's Day because they can pull practical jokes on those of us who tend to take life so very seriously—making us into their April Fools.

And many of us find the hoaxes and jokes, so, well, childish.

Oh sure, we can be as grown up and mature as the best of them. We can be serious and intense and worry our heads off. We can succumb to "work before play", easily recalling the echoes of "You have to clean your room before you go outside!" And far too often, we can get caught up in life's drudgery and feel the weight of responsibility on our shoulders.

But what if we allowed some fun, play, and foolishness into our lives? What if our Inner Child was given permission to appear, even if only occasionally?

What if we loosened our need to appear mature and so darn serious? What if we stuck out our tongues or put Silly Putty on our noses or twirled around until we got wonderfully dizzy?

How would our lives change? There are wonderful benefits to embracing our Inner Child. We allow ourselves to look at life as an adventure, with so many possibilities.

We can stay younger in spirit because we refuse to conform to the social expectations for our age group.

The great gift in all of this is that we get to keep our hard-won wisdom as an adult and enjoy the abandon of being a kid. Not a bad blend.

Now It's Your Turn:

Your assignment is to laugh and celebrate foolishness throughout today. Let the child inside of you have full rein, at least for awhile.

How did that feel?

What insight did you gain about yourself?

Week 33
Use Your Values as Guideposts

"It's not hard to make decisions when you know what your values are."

Roy Disney

Values are how you express yourself in the world; they are evident in what you do and how you act. Your values are who you are, at your core. And they are neither right nor wrong. They just are.

Your values are unique to you. And most importantly, your sense of fulfillment depends upon how fully you live these personal core values, and how well your head, heart and will align.

Like run lights on a dark, foggy night, your values guide you through the murky soup, clearly marking your path into the unknown. When you need to make a choice, consider how each option honors your values. You may actually discover that some choices stomp on your values! When your values are not being honored you may feel out of sorts, that your life is not in harmony or that something is missing. The secret to leading your most fulfilling life is to consciously make choices that resonate with your values.

So what *do* you value? A way to identify some of your values is to consider what you *must have in your life* to feel a sense of fulfillment, and then determine why this is so important to you. Your answer points to your value. For example, if you must have quality time with your family, your value may be "family" or "connectedness." Note that this is one interpretation. Your response might be different. And that's okay because your values belong to you and need to be expressed in your own words.

It's very important to honor your values as you make choices in your life. This is how you stay true to the authentic you.

Now It's Your Turn:

List 3 things you *must* have in your life to feel fulfilled.

Examine why you need these items, and then describe the values they represent. (Try to use a 1-2 word phrase as the value.)

Now identify one way you can honor each value, every day. And then do it!

*Carve out and
claim the time
to care for yourself
and kindle your own fire.*

Amy Ippoloti

Week 34
Deal with It Now or Play Whack-a-Mole with the Lesson

"What one time one refuses to see never vanishes but returns, again and again, in many forms."

Susan Griffin

You know how little kids love to play peek-a-boo? They fully believe that what they can't see really isn't there. And then they are so surprised when we part our fingers and suddenly burst into their awareness!

I've known people who've carried this concept into their adult lives. While they may understand that if something is blocked from view it still exists, they continue to believe that if they don't deal with something, it will just "disappear" from their lives.

Think how much easier life would be if that were a universal truth.

But life has a way of continually presenting you with a lesson you need to learn —again and again—until you finally get it. Ignoring the lesson or hoping that it will go away only prolongs the education, and perhaps the pain.

And you don't have to do this alone. There are lots of mechanisms out there to help you through the learning: friends, coaches, and counselors...you get the idea.

So you have a choice: deal with it now, or play whack-a-mole with the lesson.

Now It's Your Turn:

What situation keeps popping up for you in various ways?

What is life trying to teach you?

What would help you deal with this, once and for all? Name the first step you will take and find someone to hold you accountable for doing it.

Week 35
Seek Opportunities

*"The golden opportunity you are seeking is in yourself.
It is not in your environment; it is not in luck or chance,
or the help of others; it is in yourself alone."*

Orison Swett Marden

So many people believe that luck or opportunity only come to certain people because they were in the right place at the right time. I believe that's bunk.

Opportunity comes from paying attention to everything around you, no matter how far-removed the subject is from your areas of interest or expertise. Be open to new ideas, even half-baked ones because an opportunity may lurk there. Look for problems or challenges you or others are having, knowing that an opportunity for a solution may be hiding in the shadows.

The key point here is that you *make yourself ready* for potential opportunity to show up by being very curious about the world. Opportunities are all around you. Look at how to improve things or how you can build on someone else's idea. Ask yourself how to turn a challenge into a positive. Network with a diverse group of people. Offer to help others, emphasizing your unique skills, which may turn into a springboard of opportunity.

Sure, some possibilities and ideas may fall into your lap. So be grateful for those circumstances. But more often than not, make yourself ready for opportunity!

When you find something interesting, ask some preliminary questions:
* Is this something I want to tackle?
* Why do I want to spend my limited energy here?
* Do I have the time and other resources to take advantage of it?

Once you're clear on your intentions and goal, then you can move forward developing your opportunity.

And an opportunity does not have to be earth shattering. Take that stressor off the table. According to Merriam-Webster, opportunity means only that there is a favorable combination of circumstances, time and place. What you do with that is up to you.

Now It's Your Turn:

What can you do to become more aware of potential opportunities?

When an opportunity shows up, how do you recognize it?

What's your process for deciding if you'll take the opportunity?

Week 36
Simplify Your Life

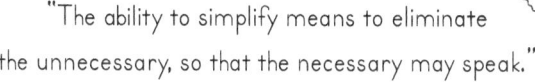

"The ability to simplify means to eliminate the unnecessary, so that the necessary may speak."

Hans Hofmann

I have been in this minimizing, clean-out mode for the past few months. At first I would carefully consider every item: keep or toss? Seemed straightforward enough. Yet, somehow a "decide later" pile kept growing. Sadly, I wasn't making the kind of progress I had envisioned.

I kept plugging along, knowing that I really had to get rid of some things. So I gave away the clothes that were never, ever going to fit me again. They were too big! Keeping them around would only remind me of my former, larger self.

And then I added those things that no longer support who I am right now. Adios to books on topics that had once interested me. Farewell to trophies—yes trophies—for events that had happened nearly 40 years ago. Good riddance to things I was "going to get to" once upon a time. And, goodbye to the associated guilt.

Suddenly I have picked up momentum. I have become more ruthless in what I am discarding. And the more I have eliminated, the more free and unencumbered I feel. There is more space in my home, and in my being. I am clearing out what no longer serves me or supports me in who I want to be in the world.

I feel such a sense of lightness and possibility. It's as if I have made space so that something new, perhaps never dreamed of, can make its way into my heart. Now, if I could just control my impatience to know what the "something" is.

Now It's Your Turn:

What no longer serves you in your life? Think about your possessions, your friends, your social activities, the causes you support, etc.

When was the last time you actually stopped to consider if these items still serve you?

What opportunities might open up if you eliminated what no longer satisfies you?

Gratitude Exercise

"Gratitude neutralizes the effects of the hedonic treadmill. It offers perspective and reminds us that there's good in our lives regardless of things that fluctuate like work, health, and relationships. When we practice gratitude for what we have, that joy and contentment stays with us a little longer."

Holstee

Why is this true for you?

Week 37
Establish Personal Boundaries

"Whatever you are willing to put up with is exactly what you will have."

Anonymous

Personal boundaries are a vital and important part of your self-care because they clarify how you will let others treat you. Boundaries allow you to determine what is acceptable and unacceptable behavior from others. It's a way to maintain self-respect and demand respect in return.

So often we say, "Yes" when we mean "No". We let people walk all over us and our needs or we don't stand up for ourselves. Maybe we sacrifice our time, energy and resources to help others, while ignoring our own lives and priorities. We become too compliant, afraid that others won't like us unless we give in.

And all of this leaves us feeling resentful, emotionally drained, exhausted and maybe even crazy.

Fact: setting boundaries is not about trying to control other people. It's about what you will and will not allow into your life, and communicating this information to others. It's about standing your ground and recognizing that your needs are important, too. It's about demanding respect from others and following through on consequences if they disregard your boundaries.

Another important point: your boundaries can change over time. They do not have to be set into concrete. Circumstances change. Our perspectives change. And, so too, can our boundaries. We just need to be clear on why we are changing them.

And, yes, some people may fall away as a result of honoring your boundaries, but you will have gained self-reliance, self-confidence and trust in yourself.

Priceless gifts!

Now It's Your Turn:

When have you said, "YES" when you really meant, "NO"?

Why did you make that choice?

What were you afraid would happen if you had spoken your mind?

What personal boundary could you create to prevent this in the future?

Week 38
Let Go of Worry

"Worry is like a rocking chair:
it gives you something to do but never gets you anywhere."

Erma Bombeck

Ever have one of those nights when you just can't fall asleep? Toss. Turn. Rollover. Repeat.

The clock on the nightstand continues its relentless path toward the hour of reckoning, just a few short digital "ticks" away. You watch the minutes flip by, desperately trying to relax and let go. The harder you try, the more awake you become.

Eventually and mercifully you do fall asleep, though it's not deep or restful. And then the buzzer sounds, the snooze button is slammed (perhaps several times?) and you suddenly realize that you absolutely Must. Get. Up. Now.

What's going on here?

So often, just as people relax and begin to settle in for sleep, their brain kicks into overdrive. All the worries of the day begin to moan for attention. They swirl around, often growing in size, incessantly broadcasting dire messages across the screen in their heads.

No wonder you can't sleep!

What would happen if you put your worries to bed before *you* crawl into bed? What if you kissed them goodnight, reassured them you'd see them in the morning, and then gently closed the door behind you?

You can do this! Simply create a worry box—any kind of container will do. And, as part of your bedtime ritual, write each worry on a piece of paper, and then say goodnight to it. Drop it into the container and *let go*.

Ahhhhhhhhhhh.

Now It's Your Turn:

What does letting go mean to you?

What sensations do you notice when you do this?

Build your letting-go muscle by choosing something to release, every day for a week. What has shifted inside you? What changes do you notice?

Week 39
Manage Your Inner Critic

*"Our doubts are traitors and
make us lose the good we oft might win,
by fearing to attempt."*

William Shakespeare

Has your Inner Critic ever dropped by uninvited? It often causes a huge nosedive from self-confidence to self-doubt, tying you up in knots and making you feel totally inadequate.

It craves the spotlight and emphasizes the "yes, but's . . . ," the "should's," and the "you're not good enough . . ." messages that tend to appear whenever you consider changing something in your life.

It has only one job: to protect you from yourself by intervening when you venture beyond your current reality.

Your Inner Critic is that voice that constrains you from living your most fulfilling, value-filled life. It allows you to live comfortably with self-limiting beliefs. It wants you to keep the status quo. It keeps you small.

And you no longer want to live small, do you? You're ready to wrest the controls from your Inner Critic. Time to take a stand! To have your "Oh, yeah?!" attitude kick in.

You have control over this voice. You can silence it, or ignore it. You can remind it of all of the times that you challenged yourself—and succeeded.

You *can* hit the mute button in your head.

Now It's Your Turn:

What situation causes your Inner Critic to awaken? And what does it say to you?

What would change if you replied, "Just because you say that doesn't mean it's true!" or "Who cares?"

What will you do, how will you be, or what will you remember to keep your Inner Critic at bay?

No one can make you feel inferior without your permission.

Eleanor Roosevelt

Week 40
Give Thanks, Often

"We often take for granted the very things that most deserve our gratitude."

Cynthia Ozick

What if today, you were just grateful for everything?

Having an attitude of gratitude is likely the most important perspective you can have. Being grateful increases your happiness, creates more positive emotions, improves your health, builds stronger relationships and helps you better deal with adversity.

Psychologists have shown that people who practice gratitude are happier and more likely to offer emotional support to others. Research also has shown that following a regular practice of gratitude and focusing on the positive aspects of your life results in a higher level of well-being. And, some medical studies indicate that giving thanks is also good for your heart! It reduces anxiety and stress and helps to keep depression at bay.

And, well, giving thanks just feels great.

Why don't you make time for it on a regular basis? Maybe the better questions are, why do you spend so much more time focusing on what didn't go right and what you don't have?

Want to start a gratitude practice? First, recognize that it's tough to start a new habit.

So, here are some ideas to get you thinking. Link your moment of gratitude to an event that already occurs for you to help jump-start your practice. Brush your teeth and think a quick prayer of gratitude for the goodness in your life. As you walk into your home, whisper, "Thanks." With each cup of coffee or tea, make a mental note of something that you are glad to have. When washing up after dinner, say "Thank you." You get the idea. Find an event that already occurs and add on a quick gratitude check in. You'll be glad you did.

Now It's Your Turn:

Make time to create a gratitude list built around the items and quantity listed here. And then notice how you feel after completing the task.

1 thing about today

2 material possessions

3 innate things

4 physical abilities you have

5 foods

6 places on Earth

7 people who have died

8 modern-day inventions

9 things about where you live

10 currently living people

How has your worldview changed?

Week 41
See Every Exit as an Entry

*"There is a trick to the 'graceful exit.'
It begins with the vision to recognize when a job,
life stage, or a relationship is over—and let it go . . .
It involves a sense of future, a belief that every exit line is an entry,
that we are moving up, rather than out."*

Ellen Goodman

Too often we view leaving something that's over like the shutting of a door. As if we now need to close off what has gone before, perhaps even nullify it and completely walk away. Over. Done.

However, you can't erase or change the past. It was. It happened. You need to validate this and understand why it was important *at the time*, which means recognizing how those events fit in with who you were *at the time*.

At the time being the key phrase.

While you may be eager to move on, you need to take time to examine how those past events have contributed to who you are becoming. Review why that relationship was important to you; why that job worked when it did; why a particular stage worked then, so you can better understand why these things no longer serve you. This doesn't mean that those events or experiences were bad, just that they no longer match *who you are now*. So you can relish how you have changed and grown and expanded.

And that is a cause for celebration! This exit is an entry to something more. You are allowing your life to move beyond the same-old, same-old. You are growing into your highest potential!

Now It's Your Turn:

How do you know when it's time to end something?

What helps you to make the leap?

What do you do to celebrate the changes you've made?

Gratitude Exercise

"'Thank you' is the best prayer that anyone could say.
I say that one a lot.
Thank you expresses extreme
gratitude, humility, understanding."

Alice Walker

How does saying "thank you" express gratitude in your life?

_____
_____
_____
_____
_____
_____
_____
_____
_____
_____
_____
_____
_____
_____
_____
_____
_____
_____
_____

Week 42
Say No to Gossip

"Gossip needn't be false to be evil—
there's a lot of truth that shouldn't be passed around."

Frank A. Clark

Ever walk into a room, you hear your name and suddenly the conversation stops and all eyes turn toward you? You probably think, "Were they just talking about me? What was that all about?" Could you have been the subject of their conversation?

That thought creates a pretty uncomfortable feeling, right? Sadly, probably everyone has gossiped at some time in their life. And more often than not, you've been guilty of passing along something negative, catty or unkind. Or maybe you've passed along some truth that wasn't yours to share.

There are lots of reasons for this kind of behavior:
* Making you feel more powerful than someone else,
* Deflecting people away from your own fallibilities,
* Helping you to feel part of the crowd or
* Getting recognition for being the one with insider information.

None of these are healthy reasons for your behavior. And they are all guaranteed trustbusters.

Remember: gossip is gossip, no matter how truthful the words are. If you don't appreciate when people gossip about you, what makes you think that it's OK for you to do it to others?

Now It's Your Turn:

Ready to take a pledge that you will no longer be seduced by gossip? Consider these proactive ideas to encourage a more gossip-free life.

1. If you find yourself continually talking about a specific person, ask yourself how this is making the world a better place.
2. Refuse to be drawn in. Shut the gossip down, kindly, perhaps saying, "I don't spread stories about other people."
3. Change the topic away from the subject of gossip.
4. Make up an excuse to remove yourself from the situation.
5. Avoid people who tend to gossip. And if you can't disconnect from them, have a conversation to work through this challenge.

How can you keep these ideas in mind as you go about your day?

Week 43
Intentionally Scare Yourself

"The danger lies in refusing to face the fear,
in not daring to come to grips with it . . .
You must do the thing you think you cannot do."

Eleanor Roosevelt

Our brains are wired to maintain the status quo. That way we can go on autopilot and conserve energy for most of our lives. Yet, where's the juiciness in that?

When we try to change the status quo, our brain begins to shout, "Danger! Danger! Unknown territory ahead!" We feel a tremendous sense of uncertainty and instability. And many of us back away because it's much safer to stay with the same-old, same-old. The status quo is so comforting.

But for those of us who are seeking some sort of change, we need courage to move forward into the unknown, untried, no-guarantee land of opportunity. This is where personal growth occurs, at the edge of our comfort zone.

And courage, like a muscle, is built one small, infinitesimal step at a time.

So, how can we create the context for nurturing courage? We can stop avoiding new experiences, letting things "happen" to us. We can speak up for ourselves, ignore the voices of others, and send our Inner Critic packing. We can surround ourselves with people who believe in us, and then truly believe what they see in us.

We can turn fear into a challenge and meet it head on. So, go for it!

Now It's Your Turn:

Be honest: what area of your life could use a courage boost? When are you afraid to step out of your comfort zone in that area?

If you could be courageous in that situation, what would change?

Now, revisit that situation in your mind, with your personal change in place. Notice what's different. What gift is there for you?

Week 44
Wake Up with a Smile on Your Face

"You've got to get up every morning with a smile on your face,
And show the world all the love in your heart."

Carole King

What if you woke up each morning with a smile on your face?

Seriously.

OK, so the reality is probably more like your hair is spiking out, you've got creases in your face from sleeping so hard, and grumpiness because you can no longer hit the snooze button.

Sound more like your reality? How about trying a different perspective?

Research has shown that smiling—even if it's not what you're truly feeling—can lift your mood. Your smile can create stress-reduction chemicals in your brain (no prescription needed). And, your smile is contagious. Just as seeing someone else yawn induces that response in us, so does smiling at another person.

Which means you're contributing to making the world a more cheerful place. Along with easing yourself into really believing that a smile is warranted.

Cool.

Now It's Your Turn:

Try this scenario: the alarm rings. You put on a smile, even if it's a fake, promising to wear that smile for 5 minutes, no matter what. Your endorphins begin to party, your mood lifts, and the day starts on a happier note.

What are you aware of?

Reflection Moment

"If not in the moment,
where do you propose to live?"

Na'ama Yehuda

What helps you live in the moment? How can you stop living in the past or fretting over the future?

_____
_____
_____
_____
_____
_____
_____
_____
_____
_____
_____
_____
_____
_____
_____
_____
_____

Week 45
Practice Civility

"Civility is not about dousing strongly held views. It's about making sure people are willing to respect other perspectives."

Jim Leach

Ah, civility.

Pretty hard to find during these polarizing times. Everyone's got an opinion, which is often shared, loudly and strongly.

And yet.

Merriam Webster defines civility as "polite, reasonable, and respectful behavior." Note the lack of qualifiers as to *when* this should occur. It doesn't mention that you need to be civil only with those with whom you agree. It's really straightforward: respectful behavior. It's a view of human beings and their inherent dignity. It's global, not situational.

Disagreement, even spirited debate, does not mean that someone is a bad person; just that they hold a different view. Period.

Is this easy? NO! Is it necessary? YES!

Civility is the glue that holds us all together. It emphasizes that we are part of a larger picture—that we have more in common than not. And it's more than good manners—it's being considerate of others by treating them as we would like to be treated. It's recognizing that *everyone is entitled to his or her own opinions*, even if those are different from our own.

I think most everyone would agree that a lack of civility is a growing problem. And that it's occurring not just in the workplace but also on social media, in our homes and communities.

So, my question is: what are you going to do about it? One thing I've learned over the years is that I only can control my own behavior. And I am going to strive for civility in all of my dealings—even if I'm facing incivility. It's the only way I can help contribute to the solution rather than the problem.

Those who look up to us are watching.

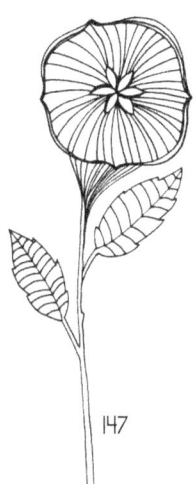

Now It's Your Turn:

When is it easy to be civil? Hard?

How can you increase the likelihood that you will practice civility more often?

Week 46
Live Without Expectations or Resentments

"Expectations are resentments under construction."

Anne Lamott

'Tis the season to have expectations: Everyone will get along. The food will be perfect. Every gift will be just what they wanted. Happiness will abound. Family members will be on their best behavior.

Ah, Norman Rockwell may be alive and well in our memories but that's not the reality of our lives around the holidays.

How often have you planned how an experience was going to unfold only to have your expectations rudely thwarted? And how often did you then let your frustrations come spewing forth onto those around you?

Why do we do this to ourselves? Why are we so certain that we know how the future will unfold? Why do we continue to believe we have so much power over life and other people?

Want a recommendation for a more peaceful holiday, whichever one you celebrate? Act as if you have no idea what will happen and revel in the adventure of not knowing. Recognize that you only can control yourself; everyone else is on their own autopilot. And what will be, will be. Relish being in the moment, however that moment turns out.

I promise you, you *can* eliminate frustration, anger, disappointment, and sadness if you just let go of any preconceived ideas about how things *should* happen.

Now It's Your Turn:

What can you let go of this holiday season?

What differences will that make to you? To your friends and family?

Week 47
Dare to Be Yourself

"We have to dare to be ourselves,
however frightening or strange that self may prove to be."

May Sarton

Have you set free the real you? Or are you stuck in presenting an image that is more likely to please others?

Far too often we automate our people-pleasing mode because we're not comfortable in our own skin. The internal voices swirl, "If they saw the real me, they'd turn away." "These are the rules I have to follow to fit in."

Notice that all of these thoughts are outward focused—as if you're seeking validation from beyond yourself. As if people's opinions are more vital than your own. Or that it's more important to be accepted by others than by you.

So, you tamp down your own personality, mute your strong points, and try to conform. You wear the plain, tailored blouse when the wild, loud, blotchy-printed top is so much more *you*.

And yet there is the tiniest voice inside that keeps saying, "Please let out the real me. Being otherwise is just so exhausting and phony."

So here's the deal: you don't have to make the world like you or validate you. You have nothing to prove! You need to trust that most people will like you *just as you are*. And, well, some just won't. Seriously, do *you* like everyone you encounter? Thought not.

If someone doesn't like you, for whatever reason that's not your problem; it's theirs.

It's more important to be genuine, true to yourself, *authentic*—the real you. It takes less energy. And comes from a place of believing, "I am enough." So, be bold, celebrate who you are and luxuriate in your uniqueness.

Oh, and if you want to wear a hot pink boa to a meeting—go for it, if that's who you really are!

Now It's Your Turn:

In what situations do you hide the real you?

What fear is holding you back from being authentically you?

How can you be just a bit bolder, and crack open the door to let out the real you?

For every minute
you are angry
you lose sixty seconds
of happiness.

Ralph Waldo Emerson

Week 48
Recharge Your Batteries

"Take time to recharge your batteries.
It's hard to see where you're going when your lights are dim."

Robert H. Conelly

Do you take better care of others than you do of yourself? Why have you made this choice? What you're really saying is that everyone else is more important than you. Isn't the true message: "I can get to everyone else's needs but I can't get to mine. I'm an afterthought. I don't deserve as much nurturing as everyone else."

Here's what's truly going on: many of us are afraid of being labeled with the S- word. You know, s-e-l-f-i-s-h. Often we believe that if we do something for ourselves, we're taking away from someone else. It's a zero-sum game. And by always putting the attention on others, it's a way of feeling "needed" or "important." It's a way of being validated—by someone else.

And yet, what is the effect of constantly doing, doing, doing for others, and not caring for yourself? Part of the answer is exhaustion, exhaustion, exhaustion, and dead batteries. So let's re-frame the perspective.

What if we believe that by taking care of ourselves, we are better able to take care of others? By nurturing ourselves, we actually have *more*, not less, to give.

So, my challenge to you: take 30 minutes out of your day—*every day*—and spend them on yourself. What a delicious gift to give to yourself! Just a couple of rules, though: no multi-tasking, no interruptions, and no exceptions. *This is time just for you.* Use this space to recharge your batteries so you have the energy and stamina to manage your busy, busy life.

Oh, and tell those "yes, buts" to get on the next bus out of town. *You're worth 30 minutes a day!*

Now It's Your Turn:

Make a list of 7 things you can do in 30 minutes to restore yourself.

Write one item on each day of the coming week and set your intention to follow through. At the end of the 7 days, notice what has shifted within you.

Week 49
Kiss "Should" Goodbye

*"Should is my all time least favorite word.
It's this sort of guilt inducing, finger wagging word
that we use to beat up others and ourselves."*

Frank Beddor

Should. Appears to be an innocent enough word. How many times a day do you use it?

On the surface it means recommendation, advisability, obligation, expectation. But it also has an implicit definition: the *should* comes from someone else's point of view, not yours. How many times have you done something based on what other people expect?

As in, "You *should* clean the house." "You *should* bake cookies, not buy them." "You *should* lose weight." Or the reverse. "You *shouldn't* try for that more advanced job." "You *shouldn't* expect to be happy in your life." "You *shouldn't* take risks because of <fill in the blank>."

Should. It's a powerful, judgmental voice implying that you don't have your own answers.

How have you been talking to yourself lately? How about considering a shift? Making choices based on your values, not those of others.

When you feel a *should* coming on, see if one of the following phrases resonates with you and helps you discover the real motivation behind the *should*. Then pledge to let go. With practice you can replace the other voices and contrary agendas around you with your own values-based choices.

* **Whose voice is really telling me this?** Often we have unexamined values that we swallowed whole from our parents, schools, or other authority figures. Where is your should/should not really coming from? Is it still serving you?
* **Am I going to do this because it's what I've done in the past?** Often we allow old, limiting beliefs to continue to influence our choices. Or, we adhere to outdated rules we don't question. How badly do you want to change?
* **Won't <fill in the name> think I will be letting them down?** Is this just a disguise for trying to please someone? Are you trying to take care of something that really belongs to someone else? Are you being manipulated?
* **What would people think if I do/don't...?** This is really a question based on what you fear. So, what's your fear factor? Rejection? Loss of a relationship? Realizing your own power?

Growth is about learning and unlearning and shedding a past that no longer serves us. It's about reclaiming parts of ourselves that may have been cast off. The payoff: watching your own, true, inner voice grow louder. Feeling your personal power blossom, overcoming your fear of change, which will lead to a more satisfying and fulfilling life. What a benefit!

Now It's Your Turn:

Monitor how often you use "should" in a day. What does the data show?

What will help you eliminate this word from your vocabulary?

If she got really quiet and listened, new parts of her wanted to speak.

S.A.R.K.

Succulent Wild Woman

Week 50
Draw a line in the Sand

*"She decided to start setting strong boundaries
because being honest and courageous
was the kind of woman she wanted to be."*

Queenisms by Cindy Ratzlaff

"Sorry, I can't do that." "I'm spread far too thin right now." "I will not allow anyone to speak to me that way." "I need some time to think about that."

These are all statements honoring personal power. Each shows various ways of saying, "No!" firmly and politely. Every one indicates a personal boundary, stated in clear, honest language.

Could you say these things when needed? Or do you choose to let people manipulate you, hiding from confrontation, swallowing your true feelings?

Putting on the superficial, happy camper face will only leave you feeling depleted, angry and resentful because you're willingly sacrificing *your* serenity for the sake of keeping everyone happy and everything on an even keel—for others.

Yet, you can choose something different. It's *your responsibility to take care of you*. It's your job to protect your time and energy. It's your duty to determine how people treat you and to stand up for yourself when you feel someone has crossed your line.

Know what you want and don't want in your life, how people *must* treat you, and what you'll do if they don't respect these things.

So, what are the gifts in all this personal work? Respect for yourself, greater self-confidence, and certainty that you have freedom of choice.

Week 51
Awaken Your Inner Child

"We are all little girls in aging bodies.
No matter how old we are, we are still that little girl that skipped rope . . . ,
skinned knees, wore braids . . . , and ate ice cream bars . . . ."

Jo Schlehofer
(As cited in *The Next Fifty Years*, Blair, 2005)

When was the last time you went outside to play? Maybe life's gotten way too serious and "grown-up" now. Or maybe you've forgotten how to be playful. Where is your Inner Child hiding?

Just because we're aging doesn't mean we have to ignore the little girl that still lives within us.

Too many people claim that they don't have time for fun. They have *responsibilities* now; too much to do in their lives. They just can't make room for anything else. Besides, "Fun is for kids."

Too many of us are pulled in too many directions by a significant other, children, work demands, and hormonal and physical changes. No wonder our Inner Child gets lost in the shuffle. Luckily she still lives, although often buried beneath the self-imposed "should's" and "have to's."

Stop for a minute. Do you really know what delights you and gives you pleasure? You may be so wrapped up in "life" that you've forgotten. You need to tune in to that little girl that lives within you. She holds the secret.

Come out; come out, wherever you are!

Become friends with your Inner Child. She's still there, inside, hand in the air, waving, "Pick me! Pick me!"

Now It's Your Turn:

Make the time to sit quietly and think back to when you were a child. Recall some of the things you had fun doing then. Why was it fun?

How did you feel? Who did it allow you to be?

How can you make room for her in your current life?

Reflection Moment

"Time spent in self-reflection is never wasted –
It is an intimate date with yourself."

Dr. Paul TP Wong

What do you want to say to yourself on this intimate date?

_____
_____
_____
_____
_____
_____
_____
_____
_____
_____
_____
_____
_____
_____
_____
_____
_____
_____

Week 52
Bid Adieu to the Old Year

What dreams really did come true for me?

What unexpected lessons did I learn?

What did I discover about myself?

What challenge forced me to grow?

What blessings did I receive?

What will I choose to let go?

What am I proud of?

What do I need to forgive myself for?

Week 53
Set Intentions for the New Year

I give myself permission to . . .

I want to experience . . .

I will show my bravery by . . .

I choose this as my power word or phrase . . .

I promise to take care of myself by . . .

When life gets shitty, I will restore myself by . . .

I choose this as my theme song for the year . . . because . . .

What's the good of living if you don't try a few things?

Charles Schultz

WHERE DO YOU GO FROM HERE?

Congratulations! You are well on your way to a wildly fulfilling life! Hopefully the blog entries, gratitude invitations and reflective moments have helped you recognize the richness of your life and let go of what you no longer need so you can embrace life more fully.

Your personal journey has helped you to discover who you really are, and what you might change to feel more fulfilled. Hopefully the wisdom you have gathered by completing each introspective exercise has opened your eyes to new possibilities and new ways of being in the world. You have discovered the benefits that self-reflection can provide, causing you to slow down so you can actually hear your true voice and name the deepest desires you have. Only then will you be able to follow your heart and make these desires your reality. You have stopped to reflect on what you are grateful for in your life, helping you to see that you really do have many more positives than negatives surrounding you.

The time has come now to send you on your way. I celebrate your courage to be willing to explore and to be open and receptive. I believe that your strength and power will carry you through any challenges you may face. And I know, without any doubt, that your gifts will change the world.

Go forth and live your most wildly fulfilling life!

ACKNOWLEDGEMENTS

The creation of a book is never a solitary journey. So many lives have intersected to bring this publication into existence. Along the way I have been exploring what I truly want so as to experience my most wildly fulfilling life and I have come to learn that I want—and need—to make an impact, while combining self-expression, adventure and challenge in the mix. This project has certainly provided all of these elements for me.

So I want to acknowledge my gratitude for the special people who have contributed to the impact I am trying to make through this book, my workshops and my writings.

First, thank you to my loyal blog readers who have offered feedback, suggested ideas, and shared how I have touched their lives and made a difference. They have been the impetus behind the creation of _Wednesday's Wisdom_, both the blog and the book. And I love that we share an intertwined journey to becoming our best selves.

Secondly, to those of you listed here. I am grateful for the steady encouragement, uplifting my spirits when the grey skies appeared, and helping to celebrate the large and small victories.

Joycelyn Campbell, Asaera Cote, and Sarah Tevis Townes, who helped me to name, clarify and create the impact I want to make. You were right, in so many ways.

Anna Pentler and Kate Davis for the energy, joy of movement and stress release your Nia classes always provide. You bring music and connection to my life.

The insightful ladies of the Elephant Tribe. You've been there for me, always.

Powerful female role models who have shown me that soul, grit, tenacity and a vision of how things could be are the tools needed to create change.

Vincent Chavez whose wizardry conceived the style I was looking for in a creative design. Your intuition is dead on.

Bruce Laramie who recognized my inner cowgirl and captured her spirit on "film".

Those who left the party too soon but who continue to support me from above. I miss you all.

And, most importantly, Ron Fisher, my partner and best cheerleader. You are the necessary ingredient.

About the Designer

Vincent Chavez was born with a pencil in his hand. Coming from a family of artists in multiple mediums, he spent his childhood obsessed with and exploring all aspects of creativity. This spark would not fizzle, but instead would keep growing. He taught his first high school art class at the age of 12, illustrated his first college textbook at 17, shot and edited television news at 19, earned his BFA and practiced in Architecture & Interiors, helped start a music magazine, and even owned and sold a popular organic breakfast restaurant. After 16 years of adult professional life, in 2014 he finally concluded that the social norms of only pursuing one practice was quite simply not his calling and thus Clean and Simple Studios was born. It's here where he dedicates himself to creating timeless works across all mediums that engage and uplift those that interact with them. He maintains his childhood naiveté that design can, and should, make our world a better place. He currently resides in Albuquerque, NM, with his two children, two guinea pigs, and an adorable mutt of a dog. You can get in touch with him at cleanandsimplestudios@gmail.com and at cleanandsimplestudios.com.

About the Author

Robin Anderson, a post-WWII baby, was steeped in the traditions of a woman's place is in the home. In high school she learned that she could make things happen, but her early college years clouded that discovery. Then the college town where she grew up was showcased on the cover of Life magazine and in the world media following the shootings at Kent State in 1970. From that point on her worldview began to shift.

She taught school, because that's what women do. Circumstance forced her to change her career and join the corporate world, albeit still following a more traditional role. While there she began to take advantage of opportunities for breaking the mold. And, just as she began to come into her own, life took her to a college town, where she became the Professor's Wife.

But her spirit was no longer willing to be held in check by cultural expectations. She landed a job at the university, doors began to open, and suddenly there were many opportunities for making things happen. She caused change to occur in technology and business, became known for her stance on women's issues, and created a women's mentoring program, which is still going strong more than a decade later. Soon her spouse became the husband of, she grinned inwardly, and never looked back.

Then her world turned upside down. She became a widow, and while marooned in the grief, she ultimately discovered a new, stronger, more confident self. And so she set about helping other women to recognize these traits in themselves.

One thing led to another and she retired from a job she loved to the great expanse of unnamed possibilities. Challenging herself to a Vision Quest, her life purpose became clear: assisting other women with their personal growth by shining a light on their inner strength and discovering ways to honor the gifts they have been given. Seeking the appropriate skills and credentialing, she became a student yet again, and proudly earned the Certified Co-active Professional Coach (CPCC) standing.

In 2012 she and her new husband transplanted to New Mexico, which proved to be the catalyst that re-ignited her smoldering artistic creative urge. Now, in her third act, she has given voice to this inherent need for greater self-expression, devoting much of her time to photography and watercolor painting. She continues to model the importance of following a life of passion, no matter the age on a birth certificate.

For many years Robin has enabled women to find their voice and their innate power through her first book, *Reclaim Your Power! become who you were meant to be*, her Wednesday's Wisdom blog, workshops, life coaching, and publications. She has helped hundreds of women who want something more in their lives, who long to reintroduce fun and passion into their vocabulary and who hunger to reclaim the feeling of being deliciously alive.

Her current focus is empowering passionate women to boldly invent their vibrant third act.

Contact her at robin@robinandersoncoaching.com

Reviewer's Comments

Wednesday's Wisdom is a highly readable book full of opportunities to look at our lives in new ways, and to discover new possibilities for inner growth. Robin Anderson's fresh, conversational writing style goes down easy when she is encouraging us to add more happiness, fun, and celebration to our lives, as well as when she is inviting us to delve into deeper topics such as getting unstuck, dealing with fear, and offering forgiveness. After each weekly reading, she offers a series of thought-provoking questions to ponder and/or journal with. I found these questions particularly helpful for my own journey. In her introduction, Robin sets her intention as a desire to offer personal growth wrapped in bite-sized pieces, and she delivers exactly that, and so much more.

> **—Anne Marie Bennett**, SoulCollage® Facilitator/Trainer, KaleidoSoul.com

Wisdom reveals itself through generous, powerful questions throughout this pensive journey. Grab a pen and beverage of choice to dial up your inner game as Robin guides and invites you to explore the common and most-human elements of life. Her humor and realness permeate the pages while making this all about you and your self-serving evolution.

> **—Janine Graziano-Full**, CPCC, Chief Possibility Officer of Live Full Coaching, LLC, livefullcoaching.com

In *Wednesday's Wisdom – a Guide to 52 Weeks of Personal Growth*, Robin Anderson offers us with a wonderful compilation of weekly prompts that encourage personal reflection. Having followed her blog for some time, I have appreciated her wisdom and direction. This, as one succinct resource now is priceless. Anderson challenges us to shift our perspective on how we approach our daily lives in order to help us realize a higher and more fulfilling life—or as she puts it, a Wildly Fulfilling Life. Her enthusiasm towards coaching, empowering us to recognize our potential, shines through in a straightforward, gentle manner. Anderson truly knows how to inspire us to wake up and approach the world in a more genuine way.

—**Joann Johnson**, Kaizen-Muse Creativity Coach, Poet and Fine Art Photographer

Based on her popular Wednesday's Wisdom blog, Robin provides us access to a year's worth of golden nuggets all wrapped up in a bow for you to open in your own time and on your own terms. Each week you can dip into a new perspective and accompanying exercise. Some are deeply thought provoking and life changing, and others are quick, simple adjustments that can really improve your experience of your life. From creating your own sanctuary and spring-cleaning your life to choosing passion over purpose and committing to what really matters, each week brings insight and practical activities to truly engage with the information. If you are committed to living your best life and willing to do the work, *Wednesday's Wisdom* cuts to the chase and can be a vehicle to get you closer to your goals. I really enjoyed this quick read and will be
applying some of these tips in my own life!

—**Giovanna Rossi**, Executive Producer/Host, The Well Woman Show, www.wellwomanlife.com

www.ingramcontent.com/pod-product-compliance
Lightning Source LLC
Chambersburg PA
CBHW040312170426
43195CB00020B/2949